I0696032

MASTERING ENGLISH GRAMMAR: A GUIDE TO AVOIDING COMMON ERRORS FOR FRENCH SPEAKERS LEARNING ENGLISH

Copyright © 2023 by Marvelous O

All rights reserved

Disclaimer

The information provided in this book is intended for educational and informational purposes only. The author, Marvelous O., has made every effort to ensure that the content presented in this book is accurate, complete, and up-to-date. However, the author and publisher do not guarantee the accuracy, completeness, or usefulness of the information contained herein, and accept no liability for any errors or omissions that may be present.

The reader assumes full responsibility for using the information contained in this book. The author and publisher disclaim any liability or responsibility for any loss or damage that may be incurred as a result of using the information presented in this book. The information provided in this book is not a substitute for professional advice, and readers are advised to seek the guidance of qualified professionals in specific situations.

The author and publisher do not endorse or recommend any particular product or service mentioned in this book. Any opinions expressed in this book are solely those of the author and do not necessarily reflect the views of the publisher

No part of this book may be reproduced or transmitted in any form or by any means, electronic or mechanical, including photocopying, recording, or by any information storage and retrieval system, without permission in writing from the publisher.

By reading and using the information contained in this book, you acknowledge and agree to the terms and conditions outlined in this disclaimer.

Introduction

Learning a new language can be both exciting and challenging. As a French speaker, you may find that English grammar and usage differ from what you're used to, leading to common mistakes and errors. However, with the right guidance and practice, you can master English grammar and avoid these errors.

This book is designed to be a comprehensive guide for French speakers learning English, providing you with the tools and strategies to avoid common errors and improve your grammar skills. Each chapter focuses on a different aspect of grammar, including nouns and articles, verbs and tenses, prepositions, word order, and pronunciation. By the end of this book, you will have a solid understanding of English grammar and usage, and the confidence to communicate effectively in English.

Throughout the book, you will find clear explanations of grammar rules, as well as examples to help you understand how to apply them. In addition, each chapter includes exercises and activities to help you practice what you've learned and reinforce your understanding of the material. Whether you're studying English for work, school, or personal growth, this book will provide you with the tools you need to succeed.

Thank you for choosing this book to help you on your journey to mastering English grammar. Let's get started.

The Purpose Of This Book

The purpose of this book is to help French speakers master English grammar and avoid common errors. Learning a new language can be challenging, and grammar is often one of the most difficult aspects to master. As a French speaker learning English, you may find that English grammar rules differ from French grammar rules, leading to mistakes and errors that can affect your ability to communicate effectively in English.

This book is designed to provide French speakers with a comprehensive guide to English grammar and usage. Each chapter focuses on a different aspect of grammar, including nouns and articles, verbs and tenses, prepositions, word order, and pronunciation. By the end of the book, readers will have a solid understanding of English grammar and usage, as well as the confidence to communicate effectively in English.

One of the key benefits of this book is its focus on common errors and mistakes made by French speakers learning English. Throughout the book, readers will find clear explanations of common errors, as well as examples to help them understand how to avoid these errors in the future. Additionally, each chapter includes exercises and activities to help readers practice what they've learned and reinforce their understanding of the material.

Another benefit of this book is its user-friendly design. The book is organized in a clear and logical manner, with each chapter building on the previous one. Additionally, the book includes translations and explanations in French to help readers who are not yet fluent in English.

Overall, the purpose of this book is to provide French speakers with a practical and comprehensive guide to mastering English grammar and avoiding common errors. Whether readers are studying English for work, school, or personal growth, this book will provide them with the tools they need to succeed.

The Importance Of Mastering English Usage For French Speakers

❖ Communication: English is a widely spoken language, and it's often the language used in international communication. For French speakers looking to work or study abroad, being proficient in English can open up opportunities and facilitate communication with people from all over the world. Mastering English grammar and usage is essential for effective communication, whether it's in the workplace, academia, or social settings.

❖ Professional Advancement: English is often the language of business and commerce, and proficiency in English can lead to professional advancement and increased job opportunities. Companies that operate globally often require employees to have strong English language skills, and being able to communicate effectively in English can give French speakers a competitive edge in the job market.

❖ Academic Achievement: English is also the language of academia, and proficiency in English can be essential for academic success. For French speakers looking to study abroad or attend an English-speaking university, being proficient in English is a requirement. Additionally, many academic journals and publications are written in English, so being able to read and understand English is important for staying current in various fields of study.

❖ Cultural Exchange: English is a global language that connects people from different countries and cultures. Mastering English grammar and usage can facilitate cultural exchange and allow French speakers to connect with people from all over the world. Understanding and appreciating different cultures is important for personal growth and development, and English proficiency can help facilitate this.

❖ Personal Growth: Learning a new language is a challenging and rewarding experience. Mastering English grammar and usage can be a fulfilling accomplishment for French speakers, and it can increase their confidence and sense of personal achievement. In addition, being proficient in English can open up new avenues for personal growth, including the ability to travel, read English literature, and enjoy English media.

In Summary, Mastering English grammar and usage is important for French speakers for a variety of reasons, including communication, professional advancement, academic achievement, cultural exchange, and personal growth. By becoming proficient in English, French speakers can expand their horizons and connect with people from all over the world.

Chapter 1: Nouns and Articles

Nouns

One of the biggest challenges for French listeners trying to understand English is mastering the use of nouns. Nouns are words that refer to people, places, things, or ideas. In English, nouns can be singular or plural, and they can also be categorized as countable or uncountable. This complexity can make it difficult for French listeners to fully comprehend English speech, especially when listening to rapid conversations or technical jargon.

To help French listeners better understand English nouns, it's important to break down the various types of nouns and provide clear examples of how they are used in English speech.

Here are some Important **Types Of Nouns In English**, along with example sentences for each one:

Common Noun:

A common noun refers to a general, non-specific person, place, or thing.

For example, "book", "cat", and "city" are all common nouns.

1) *I love reading books in my free time.*
2) *The cat is sleeping on the couch.*
3) *New York City is known for its famous landmarks.*

Proper Noun:

A proper noun refers to a specific person, place, or thing, and is usually capitalized.

For Examples: "John", "Paris", and "Eiffel Tower" are all proper nouns.

1) *John is my best friend from high school.*
2) *I visited Paris last summer and saw the Eiffel Tower.*
3) *The Mona Lisa is a famous painting located in the Louvre Museum in Paris.*

<u>Abstract Noun</u>: An abstract noun refers to a concept or idea that cannot be touched or seen.

For examples: "love", "freedom", and "happiness" are all abstract nouns.

1) *Love is a powerful emotion that can change people's lives.*
2) *Freedom is an important value that many people fight for.*
3) *The pursuit of happiness is a fundamental human right.*

Concrete Noun:

A concrete noun refers to a physical, tangible object that can be seen, touched, or heard.

For Examples: "table", "car", and "music" are all concrete nouns.

1) *The table in the dining room is made of wood.*
2) *I drive a red car to work every day.*
3) *I love listening to music when I exercise.*

Countable Noun:

A countable noun refers to a thing that can be counted and pluralized.

For Example: "book" can become "books" and "dog" can become "dogs".

1) *I have three books on my bookshelf.*
2) *There are five dogs playing in the park*
3) *He bought two tickets for the movie.*

Uncountable Noun:

An uncountable noun refers to something that cannot be counted or pluralized.

For examples: "water", "sand", and "information" are all uncountable nouns.

1) *I need to drink more water to stay hydrated.*
2) *The beach is covered in sand and shells.*
3) *Can you give me some information about the job opening?*

Possessive Noun:

A possessive noun refers to something that belongs to someone or something else. It is usually formed by adding an apostrophe and an "s" ('s) to the end of a noun.

1) *My sister's car is parked in the driveway.*
2) *The cat's fur is soft and fluffy.*
3) *The teacher's desk is cluttered with papers.*

Compound Noun:

A compound noun is made up of two or more words that function as a single noun.

For Examples: "rainbow", "toothbrush", and "baseball" are all compound nouns.

1) *I saw a beautiful rainbow after the rain stopped.*
2) *Don't forget to brush your teeth with a toothbrush.*
3) *We played baseball in the park yesterday.*

Collective Noun:

A collective noun refers to a group of people or things.

For Examples: "team", "family", and "flock" are all collective nouns.

1) *The team is working hard to prepare for the game.*
2) *My family is planning a vacation to Europe next year.*
3) *A flock of birds flew over the lake.*

Gerund Noun:

A gerund noun is a verb that functions as a noun by adding -ing to the base form of the verb.

For Examples: "Swimming", "running", and "writing" can all be used as gerund nouns.

1) *Swimming is a great way to stay in shape.*
2) *Running helps me clear my mind and reduce stress.*
3) *Writing is my favorite hobby because it allows me to express myself creatively.*
4) *Singing is one of the best ways to improve your mood and reduce anxiety.*
5) *Dancing is a fun and energetic way to exercise.*
6) *Cooking is a skill that everyone should learn..*

<u>**Indefinite Noun:**</u>

An indefinite noun refers to a person, place, or thing that is not specific or identifiable.

<u>**For examples:**</u> "someone", "somewhere", and "something" are all indefinite nouns.

1) *I heard someone knocking on the door.*
2) *We need to go somewhere to celebrate our anniversary.*
3) *Can you bring me something to drink?*

<u>**Proper Adjective as Noun:**</u> Sometimes, a proper adjective can function as a noun to refer to a group of people or things that share a common characteristic.

<u>**For Examples:**</u> "French", "Catholic", and "Republican" can all be used as proper adjectives as nouns.

1) *The French are known for their love of food and wine.*
2) *My grandfather is a devout Catholic and attends mass every Sunday.*
3) *The Republican Party is one of the two major political parties in the United States.*

<u>**Material Noun:**</u> A material noun refers to a substance or material that things are made of.

❖ **For Examples**: "wood", "steel", and "glass" are all material nouns.
1) *The table is made of solid wood.*
2) *The building's frame is made of steel beams.*

The windows are made of transparent glass.

Articles

As a French listener learning English, one important topic that you will encounter is articles. Articles are small but significant words that come before a noun to indicate whether the noun is specific or general. In English, there are two types of articles: **Definite Articles** and **Indefinite Articles**.

1) <u>**Definite Articles**</u>: refer to a specific noun that has already been mentioned or is known to the listener. In English, the definite article is "the."

❖ ***For example***:
1) *The book on the table is mine"*
2) *Have you seen the movie I recommended to you?*
3) *The Eiffel Tower is a famous landmark in Paris.*

In the first example, "the" is used because the speaker is referring to a specific book that has already been mentioned. In the second example, "the" is used because the speaker is referring to a specific movie that they recommended. In the third example, "the" is used because the Eiffel Tower is a specific landmark that is known to the listener.

2) **<u>Indefinite Articles</u>:** refer to a general or unspecified noun. In English, the indefinite articles are "a" and "an." "A" is used before a noun that begins with a consonant sound, while "an" is used before a noun that begins with a vowel sound.

❖ ***For example,***
1) *I bought a new book yesterday.*
2) *An apple a day keeps the doctor away."*
3) *She wants to adopt a puppy from the shelter.*

In the first example, "a" is used because the speaker is referring to a new book in general. In the second example, "an" is used because "apple" begins with a vowel sound. In the third example, "a" is used because the speaker is referring to any puppy in general, not a specific one.

However, there are some exceptions to these rules. For example, when the noun begins with a silent "h," such as "honor," the indefinite article "an" can be used instead of "a" because the "h" is not pronounced. Additionally, in certain situations, "the" can be used as an indefinite article to indicate that the speaker is referring to a general noun, such as "the bicycle is a popular mode of transportation."

Other Types And Examples of Articles With Their Correct Usage

<u>Zero Article</u>: It is important to note that in some cases, no article is needed. This is called a zero article. We use the zero article for general concepts, abstract ideas, uncountable nouns, and proper nouns. For example, when referring to uncountable nouns such as "water," no article is needed, as in "I need water." Additionally, when referring to general concepts, no article is needed, such as "Happiness is important."

Using the correct article can be tricky, especially for non-native English speakers. However, understanding the basic rules and practicing with different examples can help improve your accuracy.

❖ **<u>Examples</u>**:
1) *Love is a beautiful feeling.*
2) *Let's go to Paris this summer.*
3) *Water is essential for life.*
4) *She is studying French at university.*

In the first example, no article is used because "love" is a general concept. In the second example, no article is used because "Paris" is a proper noun. In the third example, no article is used because "water" is an uncountable noun. In the fourth example, no article is used because "French" is an adjective modifying the noun "university."

<u>Partitive Articles:</u>

Partitive articles are a type of indefinite article used to refer to an unspecified quantity of a countable noun. In English, the partitive article is "some" or "any."

❖ **<u>Examples:</u>**
1) *Can I have some cake, please?*

2) *Would you like any coffee with your breakfast?*
3) *She needs some new shoes for the party.*

In the first example, "some" is used to refer to an unspecified quantity of cake. In the second example, "any" is used to ask if the person wants any amount of coffee. In the third example, "some" is used to refer to an unspecified number of shoes.

Demonstrative Articles:

Demonstrative articles are used to point to specific nouns. In English, the demonstrative articles are "this," "that," "these," and "those."

- ❖ **Examples:**
1) *This book is mine.*
2) *That car belongs to my neighbor.*
3) *These flowers are beautiful.*
4) *Those shoes look uncomfortable.*

In the first example, "this" is used to refer to a specific book that the speaker is holding. In the second example, "that" is used to refer to a specific car that is farther away from the speaker. In the third example, "these" is used to refer to specific flowers that the speaker is pointing to. In the fourth example, "those" is used to refer to specific shoes that are farther away from the speaker.

Generic Articles:

Generic articles are used to refer to a whole group of things or people. In English, the generic articles are "the" and "a/an."

- ❖ **Examples**:
1) *The lion is the king of the jungle.*
2) *A dog is a loyal companion.*
3) *An apple a day keeps the doctor away.*

In the first example, "the" is used to refer to lions in general. In the second example, "a" is used to refer to dogs in general. In the third example, "an" is used to refer to apples in general.

Particular Uses of "The":

The definite article "the" can also be used in specific situations, such as with superlatives, unique nouns, and geographical locations.

- ❖ **Examples**:
1) *Mount Everest is the highest mountain in the world.*

2) *The Mona Lisa is a famous painting.*
3) *The Pacific Ocean is the largest ocean in the world.*

In the first example, "the" is used to refer to a unique and specific mountain. In the second example, "the" is used to refer to a specific painting that is known to the listener. In the third example, "the" is used to refer to a specific ocean that is known as the largest in the world.

Common Mistakes And Errors in Articles

Nouns and articles are essential components of the English language. Nouns are words used to identify people, places, things, and ideas, while articles are used to indicate whether a noun is specific or general. While these two parts of speech are relatively simple, they can be a source of confusion for learners of English. In this session, We will discuss common mistakes that people make when using nouns and articles and provide tips on how to avoid them.

Using The Wrong Article: One of the most common errors is using the wrong article (a, an, the) with nouns. French speakers tend to use "the" more frequently than necessary, and sometimes omit "a" or "an" altogether. Remember that "the" is used to refer to a specific object, while "a" and "an" are used to refer to any object in general. For example, "I saw a bird in the tree" (general) versus "I saw the bird that you were talking about" (specific).

Using the wrong article or not using an article when needed can change the meaning of a sentence. Here are some examples of incorrect use of articles:

1) *I want to buy the shirt. (Incorrect use of "the" because the shirt has not been mentioned before.)*
2) *She wants to be teacher. (Incorrect use of zero article before "teacher" because it is a singular countable noun.)*
3) *Can I have an glass of water? (Incorrect use of "an" before "glass" because it begins with a consonant sound.)*

Plural Forms: In English, plural nouns are formed by adding "-s" or "-es" to the end of the word, unlike French which has several different plural forms. French speakers often forget to add the "-s" ending, or add it incorrectly. For example, "one car, two car" instead of "one car, two cars".

Irregular plural forms: Some English nouns have irregular plural forms, such as "child" becoming "children" or "mouse" becoming "mice". These can be confusing for French speakers, who may use the regular plural form instead. It's important to learn these irregular forms and use them correctly.

Forgetting To Use An Article: In French, it is common to use a noun without an article, but in English, an article is usually required. For example, French speakers may say "I need help" instead of "I need some help" or "I need the help."

Confusing Definite And Indefinite Articles: In French, there is only one definite article ("the") and one indefinite article ("a/an"). However, in English, there are two indefinite articles ("a" and "an"), and the choice of which to use depends on the sound of the following word. French speakers may use the wrong article, such as saying "an house" instead of "a house."

Incorrect Use Of Articles With Countable And Uncountable Nouns: Countable nouns refer to things that can be counted and quantified, while uncountable nouns are used for things that cannot be counted or quantified. The incorrect use of articles with these nouns is a common mistake that many learners make.

- ❖ **Example 1:** I need some advices.
  Correction: I need some advice.
  Explanation: "Advice" is an uncountable noun, and it does not take the plural form "advices." In this sentence, we do not need to use an article before the noun because it is an uncountable noun.

- ❖ **Example 2:** She bought a furniture for her apartment.
  Correction: *She bought some furniture for her apartment.*
  Explanation: "Furniture" is an uncountable noun and does not take the indefinite article "a." Instead, we should use the plural form "some" to indicate that there is more than one item of furniture.

Incorrect Use Of Articles With Proper Nouns: Proper nouns are used to refer to specific people, places, and things. They are often capitalized and do not require articles unless they are part of a larger noun phrase.

- ❖ **Example 1**: The John is a doctor.
  Correction: *John is a doctor.*
  Explanation: "John" is a proper noun and does not require an article before it. In this sentence, "the" should be removed.

- ❖ **Example 2:** She is going to visit the Statue of Liberty.
  Correction: *She is going to visit Statue of Liberty.*
  Explanation: "Statue of Liberty" is a proper noun, and we do not need to use the definite article "the" before it. In this sentence, "the" should be removed.

Incorrect Use Of Articles With Generic Nouns: Generic nouns refer to a class of things rather than a specific thing. They are often used with indefinite articles or no article at all.

- ❖ **Example 1**: I like the dogs.
  Correction: *I like dogs.*
  Explanation: "Dogs" is a generic noun, and we do not need to use the definite article "the" before it. In this sentence, "the" should be removed.

- ❖ **Example 2**: She is a teacher.
  Correction: *She is teacher.*

<u>**Explanation**</u>: "Teacher" is a generic noun, and it does not require an article before it. In this sentence, the indefinite article "a" should be removed.

Tips For Avoiding Mistakes With Nouns And Articles:

- ➢ Learn which nouns are countable and which are uncountable.
- ➢ Understand the difference between proper and generic nouns.
- ➢ Pay attention to the use of articles in English texts, conversations, and media.
- ➢ Practice using articles with nouns in sentences and seek feedback from a tutor or native speaker.

Practice Exercises

A. The correct article (a, an, or the) or leave it blank if no article is needed:

1) ___ apple a day keeps the doctor away.
2) My friend has ___ dog that barks all the time.
3) I want to buy ___ new car next year.
4) ___ United States is a large country.
5) My sister is an artist and she loves to paint ___ beautiful landscapes.

B. Rewrite the following sentences, correcting any errors with nouns and articles:

1) He saw a accident on his way to work.
2) The teacher handed out a homework to the class.
3) She ate apple for breakfast this morning.
4) I bought book at the bookstore yesterday.
5) There are many student in the classroom.

Chapter 2: Verbs and Tenses

Verbs

Verbs are one of the most important parts of speech in the English language. They are essential for constructing meaningful sentences, as they communicate actions, events, and states of being. In this chapter, we will explore verbs in detail.

What are Verbs?

A verb is a word that expresses an action, occurrence, or state of being. It is an essential component of a sentence that provides meaning and context to the message being conveyed. For example, in the sentence "She sings beautifully," the verb is "sings," which indicates the action being performed.

Verbs are typically divided into two main categories: transitive and intransitive verbs. Transitive verbs are verbs that require a direct object to complete their meaning. For example, in the sentence "She ate an apple," the verb "ate" is transitive, and the direct object is "an apple." Intransitive verbs, on the other hand, do not require a direct object to complete their meaning. For example, in the sentence "He runs every morning," the verb "runs" is intransitive.

Verb Forms

Verbs can take different forms to indicate tense, mood, voice, and aspect. The most common verb forms in English are:

Base form: This is the simplest form of a verb, and it is used in the present tense. ***For example***, **"walk," "run," and "sing."**

Infinitive: This is the base form of a verb preceded by the word "to.**" *For example,* "to walk," "to run," and "to sing."**

Past tense: This form of the verb is used to indicate an action or event that happened in the past. For regular verbs, the past tense is formed by adding "-ed" to the base form**. *For example, "walked," "ran," and "sang."***

Past Participle: This form of the verb is used to form the present perfect and past perfect tenses. For regular verbs, the past participle is formed by adding "-ed" to the base form. ***For example, "walked," "run," and "sung."***

Present Participle: This form of the verb ends in "-ing" and is used to form the present continuous and past continuous tenses. ***For example***, **"walking," "running," and "singing."**

Verb Tenses

Verbs can also indicate the time when an action, occurrence, or state of being took place. English has twelve verb tenses, which are formed by combining auxiliary verbs with the various verb forms. The most common verb tenses in English are:

Present simple: This tense is used to describe actions or states of being that are habitual, general, or factual. For example, "She sings beautifully," and "I love pizza."

Present continuous: This tense is used to describe actions that are happening now or around the present moment. For example, "She is singing beautifully," and "I am eating pizza."

Present perfect: This tense is used to describe actions that started in the past and continue up to the present moment. For example, "She has sung beautifully for many years," and "I have eaten pizza many times."

Past simple: This tense is used to describe actions that happened in the past and are completed. For example, "She sang beautifully yesterday," and "I ate pizza for dinner last night."

Past continuous: This tense is used to describe actions that were in progress at a specific time in the past. For example, "She was singing beautifully when I walked in," and "I was eating pizza when the phone rang."

Past perfect: This tense is used to describe actions that were completed before another action in the past. For example: "She had sung beautifully before she lost her voice," and "I had eaten pizza before the party started."

Future simple: This tense is used to describe actions that will happen in the future. For example, "She will sing beautifully tomorrow," and "I will eat pizza for lunch."

Future continuous: This tense is used to describe actions that will be in progress at a specific time in the future. For example, "She will be singing beautifully at the concert next week," and "I will be eating pizza at the restaurant tonight."

Future perfect: This tense is used to describe actions that will be completed before a specific time in the future. For example, "She will have sung beautifully by the time the show ends," and "I will have eaten pizza by the time you arrive."

Verb Mood and Voice

In addition to tense and aspect, verbs can also indicate mood and voice. Mood refers to the attitude or intention of the speaker towards the action or state of being expressed by the verb. The three most common verb moods in English are:

❖ **Indicative**: This is the most common mood, and it is used to make factual statements or ask questions.
❖ **For example**:
   1) *She sings beautifully*
   2) *Do you like pizza*

❖ **Imperative**: This mood is used to give commands or make requests.

- ❖ ***For example:***
    1) *Sing beautifully*
    2) *Pass me the pizza.*

- ❖ **Subjunctive:** *This mood is used to express wishes, doubts, or hypothetical situations.*
- ❖ **For example**
    1) *If she were to sing, it would be beautiful*
    2) *I suggest that he eat pizza."*

Voice, on the other hand, refers to the relationship between the subject and the action expressed by the verb. There are two voices in English:

1) **Active voice**: In active voice, the subject performs the action expressed by the verb.
- ❖ **For example:**
1) *She sings beautifully*
2) *I ate pizza for dinner.*

2) **Passive voice:** In passive voice, the subject receives the action expressed by the verb.
- ❖ **For example,:**
1) *The song was sung beautifully by her*
2) *The pizza was eaten* by me for dinner.

In conclusion, Verbs are essential components of sentences that provide meaning and context to the message being conveyed. They can indicate tense, aspect, mood, and voice, and can take different forms depending on the situation. Understanding verbs and their various forms and functions is crucial for effective communication in the English language.

Phrasal Verbs

Phrasal verbs are multi-word verbs that consist of a main verb and a particle. They are commonly used in English and can be challenging for non-native speakers to master. Understanding and using phrasal verbs correctly is an important aspect of English language proficiency.

Phrasal verbs can be separable or inseparable. Separable phrasal verbs have the particle placed after the object of the verb, while inseparable phrasal verbs have the particle attached to the verb. For example,

"turn on" is a separable phrasal verb, as in "I turned on the light," while "look after" is an inseparable phrasal verb, as in "I looked after my sister when she was sick."

Phrasal verbs can be formed with a wide range of words, including prepositions, adverbs, and verbs. Some common words include "up," "out," "in," "off," "over," "down," "on," and "away."

<u>Common Phrasal Verbs</u>
Here are 30 common phrasal verbs and their meanings:
1. Look up - to search for information
2. Give up - to stop doing something

3. Come up with - to think of an idea or solution

4. Put off - to delay or postpone

5. Take off - to remove or start to fly

6. Get on - to board a vehicle or to have a good relationship

7. Turn down - to reject or refuse an offer

8. Look forward to - to anticipate or be excited about something

9. Break down - to stop working or to have an emotional outburst

10. Run into - to meet unexpectedly

11. Bring up - to raise a topic or child

12. Set up - to establish or arrange

13. Call off - to cancel

14. Work out - to exercise or to solve a problem

15. Hold on - to wait or to grasp tightly

16. Catch up - to reach the same level as others

17. Stand up - to rise from a seated position

18. Figure out - to understand or solve a problem

19. Give in - to surrender or yield

20. Break up - to end a relationship or to separate into smaller pieces

21. Take after - to resemble a family member

22. Bring about - to cause or make something happen

23. Turn up - to increase or to arrive unexpectedly

24. Show off - to display or boast about something

25. Give away - to give something for free or to reveal a secret

26. Pick up - to collect or to improve a skill

27. Look after - to take care of someone or something

28. Put up with - to tolerate or endure something unpleasant

29. Run out of - to use all of something and have none left

30. Get over - to recover from an illness or to move on from a difficult situation.

1. Can you look up the phone number for me?
2. I had to give up smoking for my health.

3. She came up with a brilliant idea for the project.

4. Let's put off the meeting until next week.

5. The plane took off from the runway smoothly.

6. I get on well with my colleagues at work.

7. The company turned down my job application.

8. I'm really looking forward to the weekend.

9. The car broke down on the highway.

10. I ran into my old friend at the supermarket.

11. Please bring up the topic at the next meeting.

12. We need to set up a meeting with the clients.

13. The concert was called off due to bad weather.

14. I work out at the gym three times a week.

15. Hold on, I'll be with you in a minute.

16. I need to catch up on my emails before the weekend.

17. She stood up to speak at the conference.

18. I'm trying to figure out how to solve this problem.

19. He refused to give in to their demands.

20. My girlfriend and I broke up last month.

By using phrasal verbs in sentences, you can practice using them in context and improve your ability to use them correctly in conversation or writing.

Practice Exercise
1. Complete the sentences with the appropriate phrasal verb:

a)   I need to ___________ the meeting until next week. (put off/put on)
b)   She ___________ with her boyfriend last night. (broke up/broke down)
c)   Can you ___________ the music, please? (turn up/turn off)
d)   I always ___________ my shoes before I go into the house. (take off/take on)

2. *Rewrite the sentences using a phrasal verb:*

a)   *I'll have to delay the meeting until next week. (put off)*
b)   *I stopped smoking for my health. (give up)*
c)   *I met my old friend unexpectedly at the library. (run into)*
d)   *The company rejected my job application. (turn down)*

3. *Match the phrasal verb to its definition:*

a)   *a. break up   1. to end a relationship*
b)   *b. look up   2. to find information*
c)   *c. put off   3. to delay*
d)   *d. give up   4. to stop doing something*

4. *Fill in the blanks with the appropriate phrasal verb:*

a)   *I usually ___________ early in the morning. (wake up/get up)*
b)   *They had to ___________ the game due to bad weather. (call off/call in)*
c)   *I always ___________ my car before a long trip. (check out/check in)*
d)   *We need to ___________ a time to meet with the clients. (set up/put up)*

5. *Use a phrasal verb to complete the following sentences:*

a)   *I'm really looking forward _________ the concert next week.*
b)   *She _________ a way to save money on her rent.*
c)   *The boss _________ the proposal and said we should try again later.*
d)   *We need to _________ the party until we can get more supplies.*

By practicing these exercises, you can become more comfortable and confident using phrasal verbs in your English communication.

Tenses

Tense is a grammatical category that refers to the time when an action or event occurred. In English, there are three primary tenses: present, past, and future. Each tense has a specific form that is used to indicate the time relationship between two events or actions. In this chapter, we will explore the different tenses in English and how to use them correctly.

Present Tense:

The present tense is used to describe actions that are happening now or that occur regularly.

- ***For example:***
1) *I walk to work every day.*
2) *She eats breakfast at 7 am.*
3) *They play soccer on Saturdays*

To form the present tense, simply use the base form of the verb. In the third person singular (he, she, it), add -s or -es to the end of the verb.

- **For example:**
1) *He walks to work every day.*
2) *She eats breakfast at 7 am.*
3) *It plays soccer on Saturdays.*

Note that some irregular verbs have unique forms in the present tense, such as "go" (goes), "have" (has), and "do" (does).

Past Tense

The past tense is used to describe actions that happened in the past.

- *For example*:
1) *I walked to work yesterday.*
2) *She ate breakfast at 7 am this morning.*
3) *They played soccer last Saturday.*

To form the past tense, add -ed to the base form of regular verbs. For irregular verbs, the past tense form must be memorized, as there is no consistent rule.

- ***For example***:
- Regular verb: "walk" becomes "walked."
- Irregular verb: "eat" becomes "ate," "play" becomes "played."

Note that some verbs have the same base form and past tense form, such as "cut" and "put."

Future Tense

The future tense is used to describe actions that will happen in the future. For example:

1) *I will walk to work tomorrow.*
2) *She will eat breakfast at 7 am tomorrow.*
3) *They will play soccer next Saturday.*

To form the future tense, use "will" or "shall" (less common) followed by the base form of the verb.

 ❖ *For example:*
1) *I will walk to work tomorrow.*
2) *She will eat breakfast at 7 am tomorrow.*
3) *They will play soccer next Saturday.*

Note that there are other ways to express the future tense, such as using the present tense with a future time marker ("I'm leaving tomorrow"), or using "going to" plus the base form of the verb ("I'm going to walk to work tomorrow").

Perfect Tenses

In addition to the primary tenses, there are also perfect tenses in English. The perfect tenses are formed by using "have" or "has" (present perfect), "had" (past perfect), or "will have" (future perfect) followed by the past participle form of the verb. The past participle form is typically formed by adding -ed to regular verbs, or by using the irregular form for irregular verbs.

- *For example:*
- **Present Perfect**: "I have walked to work every day this week."
- **Past Perfect:** "By the time I arrived, he had already left."
- **Future Perfect**: "By this time next week, I will have finished my project.

Tense is a crucial aspect of English grammar that allows us to express the time relationship between two events or actions. The present, past, and future tenses are the primary tenses in English, and they are used to describe actions that are happening now, happened in the past, or will happen in the future, respectively. Perfect tenses are formed by using "have" or "has" (present perfect), "had" (past perfect), or "will have" (future perfect) followed by the past participle form of the verb. The perfect tenses are used to describe completed actions or events that have a connection to the present or future.

It's important to use the correct tense when speaking or writing in English, as it can affect the clarity and accuracy of your communication. Using the wrong tense can cause confusion and misunderstandings. It's also essential to understand the different forms of irregular verbs in each tense, as irregular verbs do not follow the standard rules of adding -ed to form the past tense.

In addition to the basic tenses, there are also **Progressive Tenses** and **Perfect Progressive Tenses**, which indicate ongoing or continuous actions. These tenses are formed by using "be" or "been" plus the present participle (-ing form) of the verb, or "have been" plus the present participle of the verb, respectively.

- **Present Progressive:** "I am walking to work right now."
- **Past Progressive:** "He was eating breakfast when I arrived."
- **Future Progressive:** "I will be driving to work at 8 am tomorrow."
- **Present Perfect Progressive**: "I have been working on this project all day."
- **Past Perfect Progressive**: "She had been studying for the exam for weeks before she finally took it."

- **Future Perfect Progressive:** "By this time next year, we will have been living in our new house for a year."

Common Mistakes And Errors

French and English are both part of the Indo-European language family, but they have different grammar rules and structures, which can lead to errors when French speakers learn English. Here are some common errors in verbs and tenses that French speakers often make, along with examples of each:

Using The Wrong Verb Form:

French has several different verb forms, and it can be easy to mix them up with English verb forms.

❖ **For Example:**
1) *I have been living in Paris since two years. (should be "**I have been living in Paris for two years**")*
2) *She is not understanding the instructions. (should be "**She does not understand the instructions**")*
3) *He has worked here for three years ago. (should be "**He has worked here for three years**")*

Mixing Up The Past Tenses:

French has two different past tenses (passé composé and imparfait), while English only has one. This can lead to errors in choosing the correct past tense in English.

❖ **For Example:**
1) *I have visited Paris last year. (should be "I **visited Paris last year**")*
2) *When I was walking home, it was raining. (should be "**When I walked home, it was raining**")*
3) *We were watching TV when he came home. (should be "**We were watching TV when he came home**")*

Using The Wrong Auxiliary Verb:

In French, the auxiliary verb "être" is used for some verbs in the past tense, while "avoir" is used for others. English only uses "have" as the auxiliary verb in the past tense, which can lead to errors for French speakers. **For Example:**
1) *"She is gone to the store" (should be "**She has gone to the store**")*
2) *"I have been born in France" (should be "**I was born in France**")*
3) *"He has forgot his keys" (should be "**He has forgotten his keys**")*

Using The Wrong Form Of The Verb "To Be":

In French, the verb "être" is used for all forms of "to be", while in English, there are different forms depending on the tense and subject. This can lead to errors for French speakers. For example:
1) *"She is having 25 years old" (should be "**She is 25 years old**")*
2) *"They was at the party last night" (should be "**They were at the party last night**")*
3) *"I am liking this song" (should be "**I like this song**")*

Using The Present Tense Instead Of The Present Continuous Tense:

French does not have a continuous tense, so it can be easy for French speakers to use the present tense instead of the present continuous tense in English.

❖ **For Example:**

1) *"I go to school by bus"* (should be *"**I am going to school by bus**"*)
2) *"She speaks French very well"* (should be *"**She is speaking French very well**"*)
3) *"They eat breakfast at 7am"* (should be *"**They are eating breakfast at 7am**"*)

Using The Wrong Form Of Irregular Verbs:

English has many irregular verbs, and it can be difficult for French speakers to remember their forms.

❖ **For Examples:**
1) *"He buyed a new car"* (should be *"**He bought a new car**"*)
2) *"I swam in the pool yesterday"* (should be *"**I swam in the pool yesterday**"*)
3) *"She drived to the store"* (should be *"**She drove to the store**"*)

Using The Wrong Form Of Phrasal Verbs:

Phrasal verbs are a common feature of English, and can be difficult for French speakers to master.

❖ **For Example:**
1) *"I woke up at 7am and got over"* (should be *"**I woke up at 7am and got up**"*)
2) *"She looks after her sister's kids"* (should be *"**She takes care of her sister's kids**"*)
3) *"He turned off the lights and went out"* (should be *"**He turned off the lights and left**"*)

Using The Wrong Modal Verb:

French has several different conditional forms, while English only has two. This can lead to errors in using the correct conditional form in English.

❖ **For Example:**
1) *"If I would have known, I would have come earlier"* (should be *"**If I had known, I would have come earlier**"*)
2) *"If it rains tomorrow, I would stay inside"* (should be *"**If it rains tomorrow, I will stay inside**"*)
3) *"If I will have time, I will call you"* (should be *"**If I have time, I will call you**"*)

Using The Wrong Modal Verb:

Modal verbs are used to express different degrees of possibility, obligation, or ability, and French speakers may use the wrong modal verb when speaking or writing in English.

❖ ***For example:***
1) *"I must to study for the exam"* (should be *"**I have to study for the exam**"*)
2) *"He can to speak Spanish fluently"* (should be *"**He can speak Spanish fluently**"*)
3) *"They should to arrive on time"* (should be *"**They should arrive on time**"*)

Using The Wrong Form Of The Verb "To Do":

The verb "to do" is used as an auxiliary verb in English to form questions and negatives, and it can be tricky for French speakers to remember the correct form to use.

❖ **For Example:**
1) **Do you have a pencil?"** *(correct)*
❖ *"Have you a pencil?"* (incorrect)

2) *I don't like coffee (correct)*

❖ *"I not like coffee" (incorrect)*

3) *Did they go to the concert? (correct)*

❖ *"They did go to the concert?" (incorrect)*

By paying attention to these common errors and practicing using the correct forms of verbs and tenses, French speakers can improve their English language proficiency and avoid these mistakes in the future.

Practice Exercises

1. **Fill in the blanks with the correct form of the verb in parentheses:**

a) *She (study) for her exams right now.*

b) *I (not like) spicy food.*

c) *They (go) to the beach every summer.*

d) *He (not be) here yesterday.*

e) *We (watch) a movie tonight.*

2. **Rewrite the sentences using the present continuous tense:**

a) I read books every day. (I am ______________ books every day.)

b) She drinks coffee in the morning. (She is ______________ coffee in the morning.)

c) They play soccer on the weekends. (They are ______________ soccer on the weekends.)

d) He watches TV in the evening. (He is ______________ TV in the evening.)

e) We listen to music while we work. (We are ______________ to music while we work.)

3. **Choose the correct modal verb to complete the sentences:**

a) I ______________ go to the store later. (should / could / would)

b) He ______________ play guitar when he was younger. (can / could / will be able to)

c) They ______________ come to the party if they have time. (will / might / may)

d) She ______________ have forgotten her keys at home. (must / could / should)

e) We ______________ have dinner together next week. (should / could / must)

4. **Fill in the blanks with the correct form of the verb "to do":**

a) __________ you like ice cream? (Do / Does / Did)

b) __________ they study English at school? (Do / Does / Did)

c) I __________ my homework every day. (do / does / did)

d) We __________ have time to watch a movie tonight. (do not / does not / did not)

e) __________ he go to the gym on weekends? (Do / Does / Did)

By practicing these exercises, French speakers can improve their understanding and use of verbs and tenses in English.

Chapter 3: Prepositions

Prepositions are words that connect nouns or pronouns to other words in a sentence, indicating the relationship between the two. They usually come before a noun or pronoun and show the relationship of the noun or pronoun to other words in the sentence.

Common prepositions include in, on, at, by, with, to, from, for, and of. However, there are many other prepositions that are used in the English language.

Function of Prepositions

Prepositions have a variety of functions in a sentence, including showing location, time, manner, and relationship.

- ❖ **Location**: Prepositions can show where something is located or the direction it is moving.
- ❖ ***Examples***:
1) *The cat is on the table.*
2) *The bird flew over the house.*
3) *The ball rolled under the couch.*

- ❖ **Time**: Prepositions can show when something happened or for how long.
- ❖ ***Examples***:
1) *We will meet at 6 pm.*
2) *They have been studying for hours.*
3) *He was born in 1990.*

- ❖ **Manner**: Prepositions can show how something is done or the method used.
- ❖ ***Examples***:
1) *She brushed her hair with a comb.*
2) *He spoke to her in a gentle tone.*
3) *They ran for exercise.*

- ❖ **Relationship**: Prepositions can show the relationship between two nouns or pronouns.
- ❖ ***Examples***:
1) *The book belongs to the library.*
2) *The key is for the door.*
3) *The gift is from my friend.*

Common Prepositions and Their Uses

Prepositions are an important part of any language, including English. They are used to show the relationship between a noun or pronoun and other words in a sentence. Prepositions can be tricky for French listeners who are learning English because they often don't have a direct translation in French. In this chapter, we will go over some of the most common prepositions in English and how to use them correctly.

In: Used to show location inside a place, time within a period or duration, or a shape or color.

❖ ***Examples***:
1) *The cat is in the box.*
2) *We will arrive in an hour.*
3) *The dress is available* in blue.

On: Used to show location on a surface, time on a day or date, or to show connection to something.

❖ ***Examples***:
1) *The book is on the table.*
2) *We will meet on Tuesday.*
3) *I'm on your side.*

At: Used to show location at a specific point, time at a specific moment, or to show an event.

❖ ***Examples***:
1) She is at the store.
2) We will meet at 7 pm.
3) I am good at soccer.

By: Used to show time, method, or the person responsible for doing something.

❖ ***Examples***:
1) *I will be home by 6 pm.*
2) *She traveled by train.*
3) *The report was written by me.*

With: Used to show the manner, instrument or companion of an action.

❖ ***Examples***:
1) *She writes with a pen.*
2) *He went with his friends.*
3) *We celebrate with cake.*

To: Used to show destination, purpose or direction.

❖ ***Examples***:
1) We are going to the park.

2) He gave the book to the teacher.

3) I am studying to become a doctor.

From: Used to show the origin, source or the starting point of something.

❖ ***Examples***:

1) *She is from Italy.*
2) *The gift is from my mother.*
3) *We drove from New York to Miami.*

For: Used to show the purpose or duration of an action or activity.

❖ ***Examples***:

1) *I bought this dress for a wedding.*
2) *They have been studying for three hours.*
3) *She works for a non-profit organization.*

Of: *The preposition "of" is used to indicate a relationship or possession.*

❖ ***For Example:***

1) *The city of Paris is beautiful.*
2) *The color of the sky is blue.*

About: *The preposition "about" is used to indicate the topic of something*

❖ ***For Example:***

1) *We are talking about the weather.*
2) *The book is about history.*

Common Mistakes And Errors Made By French Speakers With Prepositions

Prepositions are one of the trickiest parts of learning a new language. Even for native speakers, prepositions can be challenging because they don't always follow strict rules and their use can vary depending on context. For French speakers learning English, there are a number of common mistakes and errors that are made when using prepositions. In this article, we will look at some of the most common mistakes and offer tips on how to avoid them.

1) Confusing "In" And "On"

One of the most common mistakes that French speakers make is confusing the prepositions "in" and "on". This is likely due to the fact that in French, the preposition "dans" can be used to indicate both "in" and "on".

However, in English, "in" is used to indicate a location or enclosed space, while "on" is used to indicate a surface or a specific day.

- ❖ ***For Example:***
- ➢ **Correct**: The book is on the table.
- ➢ **Incorrect**: The book is in the table.

2) Using "for" instead of "since"

Another common mistake is using the preposition "for" instead of "since" when talking about duration of time. While "for" is used to indicate a period of time, "since" is used to indicate a specific point in time.

- ❖ ***For Example:***
- ➢ **Correct**: I have been studying English since last year.
- ➢ **Incorrect**: I have been studying English for last year.

3) Using "To" Instead Of "At"

Another mistake that French speakers often make is using the preposition "to" instead of "at" when indicating a specific place. In English, "to" is used to indicate movement or direction, while "at" is used to indicate a specific location.

- ❖ ***For Example***:
- ➢ **Correct**: We will meet at the restaurant.
- ➢ **Incorrect**: We will meet to the restaurant.

4) Confusing "in" and "at"

Another common mistake is confusing the prepositions "in" and "at" when indicating a specific time. In English, "in" is used to indicate a general period of time, while "at" is used to indicate a specific time.

- ❖ ***For Example:***
- ➢ **Correct**: The meeting is at 2pm.
- ➢ **Incorrect**: The meeting is in 2pm.

5) Using "by" instead of "with"

Finally, another mistake that French speakers often make is using the preposition "by" instead of "with" when talking about a companion or possession. While "by" is used to indicate the agent of an action or the means of transportation, "with" is used to indicate a company or possession.

- ❖ ***For Example:***
- ➢ **Correct:** I am with my friends.

> ***Incorrect***: I am by my friends.

6) Using "for" instead of "to"

French speakers may also make the mistake of using "for" instead of "to" when indicating a recipient or purpose. In English, "to" is used to indicate the recipient of an action or the purpose of an action, while "for" is used to indicate the benefit of an action or the duration of time.

- ❖ **For Example:**
- > ***Correct****: I bought a gift for my sister.*
- > **Incorrect***: I bought a gift to my sister.*

7) Confusing "at" and "to"

Another common mistake is confusing the prepositions "at" and "to" when indicating a destination. In English, "at" is used to indicate a location or place, while "to" is used to indicate movement or direction towards a destination.

- ❖ **For Example**:
- > ***Correct***: I arrived at the airport.
- > ***Incorrect***: I arrived to the airport.

8) Using "in" instead of "into"

French speakers may also make the mistake of using "in" instead of "into" when indicating movement from one place to another. In English, "into" is used to indicate movement from the outside to the inside of a place, while "in" is used to indicate a stationary position within a place.

- ❖ ***For Example***:
- > ***Correct***: He walked into the room.
- > ***Incorrect***: He walked in the room.

9) Using "of" instead of "for"

Another mistake that French speakers may make is using "of" instead of "for" when indicating a reason or purpose. In English, "for" is used to indicate the purpose or intended result of an action, while "of" is used to indicate a relationship or possession.

- ❖ ***For Example:***
- > ***Correct****: She went to the gym for exercise.*
- > ***Incorrect****: She went to the gym of exercise.*

Practice Exercises

Exercise 1

Complete the sentences with the correct preposition: in, on, at, for, to, since, with, into, of, by.

1) The book is _________ the shelf.
2) The meeting is scheduled _________ 10am.
3) She is going _________ the party _________ her friends.
4) I have been studying English _________ six months _________ last year.
5) He walked _________ the room and sat _________ the chair.
6) I bought a gift _________ my mom _________ Mother's Day.
7) She arrived _________ the airport _________ a taxi.
8) The car crashed _________ the tree _________ the side of the road.
9) He is allergic _________ peanuts.
10) The letter was sent _________ email.

Exercise 2

Rewrite the following sentences to correct the preposition mistakes.

1) She is living in France from two years.
2) I will meet you to the park.
3) The concert is in 7pm.
4) He jumped in the pool
5) I am by my sister's house.

Exercise 3

Write a short paragraph (5-6 sentences) about a recent event or experience using the correct prepositions

For example: "Last weekend, I went to a concert with my friends. We arrived at the venue at 7pm and waited in line for an hour. Once we got inside, we found seats in the front row. The band played their new album and we sang along with the crowd. After the concert, we went to a nearby bar and had a few drinks before going home."

Chapter 4: Word Order

Word order is an essential aspect of any language, including English. The way we arrange words in a sentence affects how we communicate our thoughts and ideas to others. In Chapter 4, we will explore the various word orders in English and how they impact sentence structure and meaning.

Subject-Verb-Object (SVO) Word Order

The most common word order in English is Subject-Verb-Object (SVO). This word order is used in declarative sentences, which make a statement or express a fact. For example: "John ate the pizza." In this sentence, "John" is the subject, "ate" is the verb, and "pizza" is the object.

In SVO word order, the subject typically comes before the verb, and the object follows the verb. However, there are exceptions to this rule. For instance, in questions, the word order is often inverted, with the verb coming before the subject. ***For Example***: "**Did John eat the pizza?**"

Subject-Object-Verb (SOV) Word Order

Another common word order in English is Subject-Object-Verb (SOV). This word order is used in languages such as Japanese, Korean, and Turkish. In English, SOV word order is typically used for emphasis or to sound poetic. ***For Example:*** "**The pizza John ate.**"

In SOV word order, the subject comes before the object, and the verb comes last. While this word order is less common than SVO, it is still important to be familiar with it, especially when reading literature or poetry.

Verb-Subject-Object (VSO) Word Order

Verb-Subject-Object (VSO) word order is used in languages such as Welsh, Arabic, and Irish. In English, VSO word order is typically used in questions or in sentences that express surprise or disbelief. ***For Example***: "**Is John eating the pizza?**" or "**Eating the pizza, John is!**"

In VSO word order, the verb comes before the subject, and the object follows the verb. This word order can be challenging for non-native English speakers to master, but it is an important aspect of the language to understand.

Other Word Orders

While SVO, SOV, and VSO are the most common word orders in English, there are other word orders that are less common but still important to understand. For example, Subject-Verb (SV) word order is used in imperative sentences, which give commands or instructions. ***For Example:*** "**Eat the pizza!**"

Adverb placement can also impact word order. For instance, when an adverb is used at the beginning of a sentence, the subject and verb are inverted. ***For Example:*** "**Yesterday, John ate the pizza.**"

Word Order for French Listeners Who Want to Learn English

One of the biggest challenges for French listeners learning English is understanding the correct word order. Unlike French, which has a more flexible word order, English has a strict subject-verb-object (SVO) word order. In this chapter, we will discuss the basic rules of word order in English and how to apply them in different contexts.

Basic Word Order

In English, the basic word order is subject-verb-object (SVO). This means that the subject comes first, followed by the verb and then the object.

- ❖ ***For Example:***
1) She (subject) is eating (verb) an apple (object).

- ❖ **This Word Order Applies To Both Affirmative And Negative Sentences:**
2) He (subject) does not (negation) like (verb) broccoli (object).

- ❖ **In Questions, The Word Order Is Inverted, With The Auxiliary Verb Or Modal Verb Coming Before The Subject:**
3) Do (auxiliary verb) you (subject) like (verb) pizza (object)?

Adverb Placement

- o **In English, Adverbs Usually Come After The Verb, But Before The Object:**
1) She (subject) is eating (verb) an apple (object) slowly (adverb).

- o **If There Is No Object, The Adverb Comes After The Verb:**
2) She (subject) is eating (verb) slowly (adverb).

- o **In questions, the adverb usually comes after the subject:**
3) How (adverb) does (auxiliary verb) he (subject) speak (verb) French (object)?

Prepositional Phrases

- o **In English, Prepositional Phrases Usually Come After The Verb And Object:**

1) He (subject) is going (verb) to the store (prepositional phrase).

- o **In Questions, Prepositional Phrases Usually Come After The Subject:**
2) Where (preposition) is (auxiliary verb) the library (object)?

Complex Sentences

In Complex Sentences, The Word Order Can Be More Complicated. Here Are Some Examples:

1) Although (subordinating conjunction) she (subject) is tired (verb), she (subject) is still studying (verb).
2) Because (subordinating conjunction) he (subject) missed (verb) the bus (object), he (subject) was late (verb).

In these sentences, the subordinate clause (although she is tired, because he missed the bus) comes before the main clause (she is still studying, he was late).

In conclusion, the basic word order in English is subject-verb-object (SVO), with adverbs and prepositional phrases coming after the verb and object. In questions, the word order is inverted, with the auxiliary verb or modal verb coming before the subject. In complex sentences, the subordinate clause comes before the main clause. By understanding these basic rules, French listeners can improve their understanding of English sentence structure and communicate more effectively in English.

Common Word Order Mistakes

Here are some common word order mistakes that French listeners might make when learning English:

1) **Placing Adverbs In The Wrong Position**: Adverbs should be placed before the verb they modify. For example, "She quickly ran to the store" is correct, while "She ran quickly to the store" is incorrect.

2) **Using The Wrong Word Order In Questions:** In English, questions typically use the auxiliary verb before the subject. For example, "Did you go to the store?" is correct, while "You did go to the store?" is incorrect.

3) **Inverting The Subject And Verb In Declarative Sentences**: In English, the subject comes before the verb in declarative sentences. For example, "She is studying for her exam" is correct, while "Is she studying for her exam?" is a question.

4) **Misplacing Prepositional Phrases:** Prepositional phrases should be placed near the noun or pronoun they modify. For example, "The cat on the couch is sleeping" is correct, while "On the couch the cat is sleeping" is incorrect.

By being aware of these common mistakes and practicing to avoid them, you can improve your word order skills and communicate more effectively in English.

Here are some tips for improving your word order skills in English:

- ➢ **Read And Listen To English**: Reading and listening to English materials, such as books, news articles, and podcasts, can help you become more familiar with the proper word order in English.

- ➢ **Practice Writing And Speaking**: Practice forming sentences with correct word order and asking questions in English. This will help you develop a better understanding of the rules and apply them in real-life situations.

- ➢ **Pay Attention To Word Order In Context:** Pay attention to the word order used in different contexts, such as in different tenses, in questions, and in complex sentences. This will help you become more comfortable with the rules and how they are applied in different situations.

- ➢ **Study Grammar Rules:** Review grammar rules related to word order and practice exercises to reinforce your understanding of the rules.

- ➢ **Get Feedback From A Native Speaker:** Getting feedback from a native speaker can help you identify and correct mistakes in your word order. You can find language exchange partners or work with a language tutor to improve your skills.

By following these tips and practicing regularly, you can improve your word order skills and become more confident in communicating in English.

- • Practice Exercises

1. ***Rearrange the following words to form a grammatically correct sentence:***
a) is / listening / to music / she / in her room
b) going / to the / park / they / are / this afternoon
c) did / you / movie / the / like / last night

2. ***Identify The Subject, Verb, And Object In The Following Sentences:***
a) The cat is sleeping on the couch.
b) John and Sarah went to the beach yesterday.
c) She is reading a book about history.

3. ***Rewrite the following sentences, changing the word order to make them questions:***
a) She is studying for her exam.
b) He ate a sandwich for lunch.
c) They will go to the party tonight.

Chapter 5: Pronunciation in English

Pronunciation in English refers to the way in which English words are spoken or articulated. It involves the correct formation of the individual sounds that make up the language, as well as the appropriate intonation, stress, and rhythm.

Accurate pronunciation is crucial for effective communication in English, as it allows the speaker to be easily understood by others. Proper pronunciation involves paying attention to the individual sounds, or phonemes, that make up words, and mastering their production, such as the correct placement of the tongue, lips, and jaw.

English pronunciation can be challenging, particularly for non-native speakers, as there are many sounds that do not exist in other languages. Additionally, English pronunciation can vary widely depending on regional dialects, accents, and even social and cultural factors.

As a French listener who wants to understand English, one of the most challenging aspects of the language is its pronunciation. English is a language with many different dialects and accents, which can make it difficult to understand even for native speakers. However, there are some key rules and tips that can help you improve your English pronunciation and better comprehend spoken English.

Sounds and Letters

The first step in mastering English pronunciation is understanding the relationship between sounds and letters. Unlike French, English is not a phonetic language, which means that the way a word is spelled does not always correspond to the way it is pronounced. This can be confusing, but there are some general rules to follow. For example, the letters "th" are pronounced as either "th" or "f" depending on the word (e.g. "the" is pronounced "thuh" while "think" is pronounced "fink"). Additionally, some letters are silent (e.g. "k" in "know") while others change their sound depending on their position in a word (e.g. "a" in "cat" versus "car").

Vowels and Consonants

Another key aspect of English pronunciation is understanding the difference between vowels and consonants. Vowels are sounds that are made with an open mouth and a vibrating vocal cord, while consonants are sounds that are made with the lips, teeth, and tongue. English has 12 vowel sounds and 24 consonant sounds, and mastering them is essential to understanding spoken English. Some of the most common vowel sounds in English include "a" as in "cat," "e" as in "bed," "i" as in "bit," "o" as in "hot," and "u" as in "cut." Some of the most common consonant sounds in English include "b," "c," "d," "f," "g," "h," "j," "k," "l," "m," "n," "p," "q," "r," "s," "t," "v," "w," "x," "y," and "z."

Stress and Intonation

In addition to individual sounds, English pronunciation also involves stress and intonation. Stress refers to the emphasis placed on certain syllables in a word, while intonation refers to the rise and fall of pitch in a sentence. English is a stress-timed language, which means that the stress on syllables is more important than the number of syllables in a word. For example, the word "photographer" is stressed on the second syllable ("fo-TOG-ra-pher"), while the word "photography" is stressed on the third syllable ("fo-tog-RA-phy"). Intonation can also convey meaning in English. For example, a rising intonation at the end of a sentence can indicate a question, while a falling intonation can indicate a statement.

More About Sounds in English

English has 44 sounds, including 20 vowel sounds and 24 consonant sounds. Understanding how to produce each sound correctly is essential for clear pronunciation. The sounds of English can be categorized into two types: vowels and consonants.

Vowels are sounds produced without any obstruction to the airflow in the mouth. They are the most important sounds in English, as they form the nucleus of every syllable. The 20 vowel sounds of English can be further divided into two categories: short vowels and long vowels. Short vowels are pronounced

quickly, while long vowels are pronounced for a longer duration.

Consonants, on the other hand, are sounds produced with some obstruction to the airflow in the mouth. They are important for forming the onset and coda of syllables in English. The 24 consonant sounds of English can be divided into two categories: voiced and voiceless consonants. Voiced consonants are produced with the vocal cords vibrating, while voiceless consonants are produced without vibration.

Examples of English sounds:

❖ **Short Vowels**

- /æ/ as in "cat"
- /ɛ/ as in "met"
- /ɪ/ as in "hit"
- /ɒ/ as in "hot"
- /ʌ/ as in "hut"
- /ʊ/ as in "put"

❖ **Long Vowels**

- /eɪ/ as in "day"
- /iː/ as in "meet"
- /aɪ/ as in "fly"

- /oʊ/ as in "go"

- /u:/ as in "you"

- /ɔɪ/ as in "boy"

❖ **<u>Diphthongs</u>**:

- /eɪ/ as in "say"

- /aʊ/ as in "house"

- /oʊ/ as in "boat"

- /aɪ/ as in "buy"

- /ɔɪ/ as in "coin"

- /ju/ as in "use"

❖ **<u>Voiced consonants:</u>**

- /b/ as in "bat"
- /d/ as in "dog"
- /g/ as in "go"
- /v/ as in "van"
- /z/ as in "zoo"

- /ʒ/ as in "pleasure"

- /ð/ as in "then"
- /m/ as in "man"
- /n/ as in "no"
- /ŋ/ as in "sing"
- /l/ as in "love"
- /r/ as in "red"
- /j/ as in "yellow"
- /w/ as in "water"

❖ **<u>Voiceless consonants:</u>**

- /p/ as in "pen"
- /t/ as in "top"
- /k/ as in "kite"
- /f/ as in "fan"
- /s/ as in "sun"

- /ʃ/ as in "shoe"
- /θ/ as in "thin"
- /h/ as in "hat"
- /tʃ/ as in "church"

As a French listener learning English, it is important to understand the basics of sounds and letters in English. Here are some sentences that explain key concepts:

English has 26 letters, but these letters can represent more than 44 sounds. This means that some letters can represent multiple sounds, and some sounds are represented by multiple letters.

Vowels are especially important in English, as they form the nucleus of every syllable. Unlike in French, where many vowels are nasalized, English vowels are pronounced without any nasalization.

Consonants are also important in English, as they form the onset and coda of syllables. English has several consonants that are not present in French, such as /θ/ as in "think" and /ʒ/ as in "vision."

English pronunciation can be tricky because many words are not pronounced the way they are spelled. For example, the word "colonel" is pronounced "kernel," and the word "island" is pronounced "eye-land."

Learning the International Phonetic Alphabet (IPA) can be very helpful for understanding and producing the sounds of English. The IPA provides a standardized way to represent each sound, and can help you identify the differences between similar-sounding words.

Practicing pronunciation exercises, such as repeating minimal pairs (words that differ by only one sound) and reading aloud, can help improve your pronunciation skills over time.

More About Stress in English

Stress is an important aspect of English pronunciation that refers to the emphasis placed on certain syllables in a word or sentence. Understanding and using proper stress is essential for effective communication and comprehension in English.

In English, there are two types of stress: word stress and sentence stress. Word stress refers to the emphasis placed on a particular syllable within a word, while sentence stress refers to the emphasis placed on certain words within a sentence.

Word Stress is determined by the number of syllables in a word and the placement of the stress within that word. There are several general rules that can help learners determine the stress pattern of a word. For example, in two-syllable words, the stress is typically on the first syllable (e.g., "water" and "table"). In words with three or more syllables, the stress is typically on the second-to-last syllable (e.g., "banana" and "computer").

However, there are many exceptions to these rules, and learners must pay close attention to the pronunciation of individual words to determine the correct stress pattern. For example, the word "photograph" has three syllables, but the stress is on the second syllable ("phoTOgraph"). Similarly, the word "important" has three syllables, but the stress is on the first syllable ("imPORTant").

Here are some examples of word stress in English that may help French listeners understand better:
1) *"hello" - the stress is on the first syllable: "HE-llo"*
2) *"banana" - the stress is on the second syllable: "ba-NANA"*
3) *"'photograph" - the stress is on the second syllable: "pho-TO-graph"*
4) *"computer" - the stress is on the second-to-last syllable: "com-PU-ter"*
5) *"syllable" - the stress is on the second syllable: "SYL-la-ble"*
6) *"chocolate" - the stress is on the second syllable: "CHOC-o-late"*
7) *"umbrella" - the stress is on the first syllable: "UM-brel-la"*
8) *"telephone" - the stress is on the second-to-last syllable: "TE-le-phone"*
9) *"library" - the stress is on the second syllable: "LI-bra-ry"*
10) *"musician" - the stress is on the second syllable: "mu-SI-cian"*

Additionally, it is important to note that in English, word stress can also change the meaning of a word. For example, consider the words "record" and "permit." Depending on which syllable is stressed, these words can have different meanings:

1. "record" - If the stress is on the first syllable, it is a noun meaning a document of information. If the stress is on the second syllable, it is a verb meaning to make a recording.

2. "permit" - If the stress is on the first syllable, it is a noun meaning an official document allowing someone to do something. If the stress is on the second syllable, it is a verb meaning to allow or give permission.

Therefore, understanding and using proper word stress is crucial for both pronunciation and comprehension in English.

Sentence Stress: refers to the emphasis placed on certain words within a sentence to convey meaning and intention. Sentence stress can change the meaning of a sentence, even if the words themselves are the same. For example, consider the following sentence:

"I didn't say he stole the money."

The meaning of this sentence changes depending on which word is stressed. If the stress is on "I," the sentence suggests that someone else said it. If the stress is on "didn't," the sentence suggests that it is untrue. If the stress is on "say," the sentence suggests that something else was communicated. If the stress is on "he," the sentence suggests that someone else stole the money. Finally, if the stress is on "stole," the sentence suggests that he did something else with the money.

- ❖ "I want to GO to the BEACH today."
  In this sentence, the stress is on the words "go" and "beach," which indicates that the speaker wants to go specifically to the beach.

- ❖ "The ANSWER to that question is NO."
  In this sentence, the stress is on the words "answer" and "no," which indicates that the speaker is providing a clear response to a question.

- ❖ "He SAID he would CALL me BACK tomorrow."
  In this sentence, the stress is on the words "said," "call," and "tomorrow," which indicates that the speaker is emphasizing the promise made by the other person to call back the following day.

- ❖ "I can't BELIEVE you're SERIOUS about this."
  In this sentence, the stress is on the words "believe" and "serious," which indicates that the speaker is expressing surprise and disbelief about what the other person is saying.

- ❖ "I'm SO excited to see you AGAIN."
  In this sentence, the stress is on the words "so" and "again," which indicates that the speaker is emphasizing their excitement about seeing the other person once more.

- ❖ "'Are you GOING to the store today or TOMORROW?"
  In this sentence, the stress is on the words "going" and "tomorrow," which indicates that the speaker is asking about the timing of the trip to the store.

- ❖ "I CAN'T believe I forgot my PHONE at home."
  In this sentence, the stress is on the words "can't" and "phone," which indicates that the speaker is expressing surprise and frustration about forgetting their phone.

- ❖ "She's NOT going to be ABLE to come to the party."
  In this sentence, the stress is on the words "not" and "able," which indicates that the speaker is emphasizing that the person is unable to attend the party.

- ❖ "We need to CLEAN the house BEFORE the guests arrive."
  In this sentence, the stress is on the words "clean" and "before," which indicates that the speaker is emphasizing the importance of cleaning the house before the guests arrive.

- ❖ "I'm INTERESTED in learning more about that TOPIC."
  In this sentence, the stress is on the words "interested" and "topic," which indicates that the speaker is expressing curiosity and a desire to learn more about the subject.

- ❖ "I'm HOPING to hear back from the job INTERVIEW soon."

In this sentence, the stress is on the words "hoping," "hear," and "interview," which indicates that the speaker is emphasizing their desire to receive a response from the job interview.

❖ "The TOWER of London is a popular TOURIST attraction."
In this sentence, the stress is on the words "tower," "London," "tourist," and "attraction," which indicates that the speaker is emphasizing the name of the famous landmark and its popularity among tourists.

❖ "I'm SORRY, I can't come to your PARTY tonight."
In this sentence, the stress is on the words "sorry," "can't," "come," "party," and "tonight," which indicates that the speaker is emphasizing their regret about not being able to attend the party.

❖ "The BLACK cat jumped over the FENCE."
In this sentence, the stress is on the words "black," "cat," "jumped," "over," and "fence," which indicates that the speaker is emphasizing the color and action of the cat and its location in relation to the fence.

❖ "The best WAY to learn English is to PRACTICE every day."
In this sentence, the stress is on the words "best," "way," "learn," "English," "practice," and "day," which indicates that the speaker is emphasizing the importance of consistent practice for improving English skills.

More on Intonation in English

Intonation: is an important aspect of spoken English that can greatly impact the meaning of a sentence. In this session, we will explore the concept of intonation in English and provide examples to help French listeners better understand how it works.

What is Intonation?
Intonation refers to the variation of pitch or tone of voice when speaking. It involves the rise and fall of the voice, and can indicate a range of meanings and emotions, including questions, statements, emphasis, and sarcasm.

Types of Intonation
There are three main types of intonation in English: **falling**, **rising**, and **falling-rising**.

Falling Intonation:
Falling intonation occurs when the voice drops in pitch at the end of a sentence. It is often used to indicate a statement, command, or declaration.

❖ *Example*:
1) I am going to the store today." (***In this sentence, the pitch of the voice drops at the end, indicating a statement or declaration of intent).***

2) I'm so tired" (***said with a falling intonation at the end to emphasize the speaker's exhaustion).***

3) I have a lot of work to do" (***said with a falling intonation to convey a serious tone and emphasis on the amount of work)***

4) The movie was really boring" (***said with a falling intonation to indicate a negative opinion)***.

5) I don't want to talk about it" (***said with a falling intonation to convey a firm decision)***.

6) I already told you" (***said with a falling intonation to indicate annoyance or frustration)***.

Rising Intonation:

Rising intonation occurs when the voice rises in pitch at the end of a sentence. It is often used to indicate a question, hesitation, or uncertainty.

❖ **Examples;**

1) Are you coming to the party tonight?" (***In this sentence, the pitch of the voice rises at the end, indicating a question and seeking a response)***.

2) You're coming to the party, right?" (***In this sentence, the speaker is seeking confirmation from the listener and using rising intonation to indicate that a response is needed)***.

3) You're from France, aren't you?" (***In this sentence, the speaker is using rising intonation to ask a question and seeking confirmation from the listener)***.

4) I think we should try that new restaurant tonight?" (***In this sentence, the speaker is using rising intonation to suggest a course of action and seeking agreement from the listener)***.

5) You're not afraid of heights, are you?" (***In this sentence, the speaker is using rising intonation to ask a question and seeking a response)***.

6) He's a great singer, isn't he?" (***In this sentence, the speaker is using rising intonation to ask a question and seeking agreement from the listener)***

Falling-Rising Intonation:

Falling-rising intonation occurs when the voice drops in pitch and then rises again at the end of a sentence. It is often used to indicate emphasis, surprise, or sarcasm.

Example:

1) I really enjoyed the movie (rising pitch) - NOT! (falling pitch)"
(*In this sentence, the pitch of the voice rises initially to indicate sincerity, and then falls to indicate sarcasm and the opposite meaning)*.

2) I really enjoyed your company (rising pitch) - we should do this again sometime (falling pitch)."

(In this sentence, the pitch of the voice rises initially to indicate sincerity and enjoyment, and then falls to suggest the idea of meeting again).

3) That's a great idea (rising pitch) - if you want to fail (falling pitch)."
(In this sentence, the pitch of the voice rises initially to indicate approval, but then falls to convey sarcasm and disapproval).

4) I can't believe you did that (rising pitch) - you're such a genius (falling pitch)."
(In this sentence, the pitch of the voice rises initially to indicate surprise or disbelief, and then falls to convey sarcasm and the opposite meaning).

5) I'm really sorry for what I said (rising pitch) - it was completely out of line (falling pitch)."
(In this sentence, the pitch of the voice rises initially to indicate sincerity and regret, and then falls to suggest the idea of having crossed a boundary).

6) It's so nice to see you (rising pitch) - what brings you here (falling pitch)?"
(In this sentence, the pitch of the voice rises initially to indicate enthusiasm or friendliness, and then falls to indicate a change in topic and the beginning of a conversation).

Uses of Intonation

Intonation can be used to convey a range of meanings and emotions, including:

1. **Emphasis**: By emphasizing certain words or phrases with rising or falling intonation, speakers can indicate the importance or relevance of certain ideas.

2. **Attitude**: Intonation can also convey the speaker's attitude towards the subject or listener, such as sarcasm or sincerity.

3. **Clarity**: By using rising or falling intonation, speakers can help clarify the meaning of a sentence and ensure that the listener understands the intended message.

4. **Questions**: Intonation is especially important in asking questions, as rising intonation at the end of a sentence indicates that a response is needed.

Common mistakes and how to avoid them in English Pronunciation

English pronunciation can be a challenging aspect for French learners. Here are some common mistakes that French learners make and tips on how to avoid them:

1. **Pronouncing The "Th" Sound As "Z" Or "S".**

The "th" sound is unique to English and can be difficult for French learners. A common mistake is to substitute the "th" sound with "z" or "s". For example, "think" may be pronounced as "zink" or "sink".

To avoid this mistake, focus on the placement of your tongue behind your teeth. The "th" sound is made by placing the tip of your tongue between your teeth and blowing air out. Practice this sound by saying words like "think", "thanks", and "thought".

2. **Confusing "V" And "W" Sounds.**
In French, the "v" and "w" sounds are pronounced similarly, which can lead to confusion for French learners. For example, "very" may be pronounced as "wery" or "weary".

To avoid this mistake, practice the difference between the two sounds. The "v" sound is made by vibrating your lips, while the "w" sound is made by rounding your lips and blowing air out. Say words like "van", "very", and "vote" to practice the "v" sound, and words like "wet", "wine", and "win" to practice the "w" sound.

3. **Mispronouncing Unstressed Syllables.**
In English, many words have unstressed syllables, which can be pronounced differently than in French. A common mistake is to pronounce all syllables with equal stress, which can make your English sound choppy and unclear.

To avoid this mistake, practice listening to and imitating native speakers. Pay attention to the stress patterns of words and the way they pronounce unstressed syllables. You can also use dictionaries or pronunciation guides to help you identify which syllables are stressed and which are unstressed.

4. **Not Pronouncing The Final Consonant**
In French, many final consonants are not pronounced, which can lead to a similar mistake in English. For example, "cat" may be pronounced as "cah", or "dog" may be pronounced as "doh".

To avoid this mistake, make a conscious effort to pronounce the final consonant in English words. Practice saying words like "cat", "dog", and "map" while emphasizing the final consonant.

5. **Overemphasizing The Accent.**
French learners may overemphasize their French accent when speaking English, which can make their English sound unnatural and difficult to understand.

To avoid this mistake, focus on imitating the pronunciation of native speakers. Listen to how they pronounce words and practice imitating their intonation, stress, and rhythm. This will help you sound more natural and improve your communication skills in English.

6. **Incorrectly Pronouncing Diphthongs.**
English has many diphthongs, which are two vowel sounds pronounced together. A common mistake is to pronounce them as separate sounds. For example, "boat" may be pronounced as "bo-at" instead of "boht".

To avoid this mistake, practice pronouncing diphthongs by saying words like "coin", "boy", and "loud". Pay attention to how the sounds blend together and practice imitating tlt he sounds.

7. **Pronouncing "R" Sounds Incorrectly.**

In French, the "r" sound is pronounced differently than in English. French learners may have difficulty pronouncing the English "r" sound, which can lead to a rolling or guttural sound. For example, "red" may be pronounced as "rehd" or "rayd".

To avoid this mistake, practice pronouncing the "r" sound in English. Start by practicing words like "red", "river", and "rain". Pay attention to the position of your tongue and the way the sound is produced in your throat.

8. <u>**Not Differentiating Between Long And Short Vowel Sounds.**</u>
In English, there are both long and short vowel sounds. A common mistake is to pronounce them all the same, which can lead to confusion and miscommunication. For example, "bit" and "beat" have different vowel sounds.

To avoid this mistake, practice differentiating between long and short vowel sounds. Practice words like "bit" and "beat", "hop" and "hope", and "cut" and "cute". Pay attention to the length of the vowel sound and practice imitating the sounds.

9. <u>**Not Using Appropriate Intonation.**</u>
Intonation is important in English, as it can convey meaning and emotion. A common mistake is to use the wrong intonation, which can make your English sound flat or robotic. For example, asking a question with a flat intonation can make it sound like a statement.

To avoid this mistake, practice using appropriate intonation for different situations. Pay attention to the rising and falling of your voice, and practice using different intonation patterns for questions, statements, and exclamations.

Tips and strategies for improving pronunciation

If you're a French learner of English, there are several tips and strategies that you can use to improve your pronunciation. Here are some of the most effective ways to do so:

1. **Listen To Native Speakers:** One of the best ways to improve your pronunciation is by listening to native speakers. You can listen to English music, watch English TV shows and movies, or even attend language exchange events. By listening to how native speakers pronounce words and phrases, you'll get a better sense of how to correctly pronounce them yourself.

2. **Practice With Audio Recording:** In addition to listening to native speakers, it's helpful to practice with audio recordings. You can use online resources, such as podcasts and language learning apps, to practice your pronunciation. By practicing with audio recordings, you'll be able to hear how you sound and make corrections as necessary.

3. **Focus On Individual Sounds:** English has many sounds that are different from French. Focusing on individual sounds can help you improve your overall pronunciation. Practice saying words that contain sounds that you

find difficult, such as "th" or "r". You can also use online resources, such as the International Phonetic Alphabet, to help you identify and practice specific sounds.

4. Mimic Native Speakers: Another effective strategy for improving your pronunciation is to mimic native speakers. Try to imitate the way they speak, including their accent, intonation, and rhythm. This will help you get a better feel for how English should sound.

5. Record Yourself Speaking: Recording yourself speaking is a great way to identify areas where you need to improve. Use your smartphone or computer to record yourself speaking English. Then, listen to the recording and identify areas where you need to work on your pronunciation. This can help you make targeted improvements to your pronunciation.

6. Get Feedback From Others: Getting feedback from others is an important part of improving your pronunciation. You can ask a friend or language exchange partner to listen to you speak and provide feedback on areas where you need to improve. You can also consider taking classes or working with a tutor who can provide more structured feedback and guidance.

Practice Exercises

Here are some exercises you can use to improve your pronunciation in English:

1. **Tongue Twisters:** Tongue twisters are a great way to practice your pronunciation, especially for sounds that you find difficult. **Try saying these tongue twisters out loud:**

- She sells seashells by the seashore.
- How much wood would a woodchuck chuck, if a woodchuck could chuck wood?
- Peter Piper picked a peck of pickled peppers.
- Unique New York, unique New York, unique New York.

2. **Minimal Pairs:** Minimal pairs are pairs of words that differ by only one sound. Practicing with minimal pairs can help you improve your ability to distinguish between similar sounds. Here are some examples:

- Ship vs. sheep
- Cat vs. cut
- Bat vs. bet
- Light vs. right

3. **Read Aloud:** Reading aloud is an effective way to practice your pronunciation. Choose a passage from a book or article and read it out loud. Pay attention to your intonation, rhythm, and stress. Record yourself reading and listen back to identify areas where you need to improve.

4. **Listen And Repeat:** Listen to audio recordings of native English speakers and try to imitate their pronunciation. Repeat what you hear out loud, focusing on your intonation, rhythm, and stress. You can use language learning apps or websites to find audio recordings to practice with.

5. **<u>Sing Along:</u>** Singing along to English songs is a fun way to practice your pronunciation. Pay attention to the lyrics and try to mimic the singer's pronunciation. You can find the lyrics to your favorite songs online and sing along with the music.

Chapter 6: Conclusion

Congratulations on completing this guide to mastering English grammar and pronunciation for French speakers! I hope that you have found it useful and that it has helped you improve your English language skills.

In this guide, I covered a range of topics related to English grammar and pronunciation. I started with the basics of English grammar, including parts of speech, sentence structure, and common errors to avoid. I, then explored the importance of stress and intonation in English, as well as the common mistakes that French speakers make when speaking English.

I also delved into the world of phrasal verbs, discussing their meanings, usage, and common examples. Through exercises and examples, I provided opportunities for you to practice and strengthen your understanding of these essential aspects of English language learning.

It is important to remember that mastering English grammar and pronunciation takes time and effort. Consistent practice, both in formal and informal settings, is key to improving your skills. Engage with English speakers whenever possible, whether through conversation groups, online forums, or language exchanges. Watch movies and television shows in English, read books and news articles, and listen to podcasts or music to expose yourself to a variety of English language contexts.

Finally, I encourage you to remain patient and persistent in your language learning journey. Language learning is a process, and it is normal to make mistakes and encounter challenges along the way. Remember that each step you take towards mastering English grammar and pronunciation is a step closer to achieving your language goals.

I hope that this guide has been a valuable resource for you and wish you all the best in your continued English language learning.

Summary Of The Main Points In The Book

The book "Mastering English Grammar: A Guide to Avoiding Common Errors for French Speakers Learning English" covers a range of topics related to English grammar and pronunciation for French speakers. The main points covered in the book include the basics of English grammar, parts of speech, sentence structure, common errors to avoid, the importance of stress and intonation in English, common mistakes that French speakers make when speaking English, and the usage and meaning of phrasal verbs. The book also provides exercises and examples to help readers practice and strengthen their language skills, and tips and strategies for improving pronunciation. Ultimately, the book emphasizes that consistent practice and patience are essential in mastering English grammar and pronunciation, and encourages readers to engage with English speakers and immerse themselves in English language contexts.

Message Directly From The Author

Dear readers,

Thank you for taking the time to read our guide to mastering English grammar and pronunciation for French speakers. I hope that you have found it informative and helpful in your language learning journey.

As I strive to continually improve our guide and provide the best possible resources for our readers, we would greatly appreciate your feedback. If you found this guide helpful, please consider leaving a rating or review to share your experience with others who may be looking for similar language learning resources.

Your feedback helps us understand what works and what needs improvement, and it also helps other readers determine if this guide is a good fit for their language learning needs.

Thank you for your support, and we hope that you continue to find success in your English language learning endeavors.

www.ingramcontent.com/pod-product-compliance
Lightning Source LLC
Chambersburg PA
CBHW081540250726
48659CB00009B/3019